# Bill Russell

by Nick Healy

 Raintree

Chicago, Illinois

For information, address the publisher:
Raintree, 100 N. LaSalle, Suite 1200, Chicago, IL 60602

Printed and bound in the United States at Lake Book Manufacturing, Inc.
07 06 05 04 03
10 9 8 7 6 5 4 3 2 1

**Library of Congress Cataloging-in-Publication Data:**

Healy, Nick.
  Bill Russell / Nick Healy.
      p. cm. -- (African-American biographies)
Summary: Profiles Bill Russell, whose career as an outstanding rebounder for the Boston Celtics led him to become the first African American elected to the Basketball Hall of Fame and the first African American to coach in the NBA.
  ISBN 0-7398-7034-3 (lib. bdg. : hardcover) -- ISBN 1-4109-0315-X (pbk.)
  1. Russell, Bill, 1934---Juvenile literature. 2. Basketball players--United States--Biography--Juvenile literature. [1. Russell, Bill, 1934- 2. Basketball players. 3. African Americans--Biography.] I. Title. II. Series: African American biographies (Chicago, Ill.)
  GV884.R86H43 2003
  796.323'092--dc21

                                2003002131

**Acknowledgments**
The publisher would like to thank the following for permission to reproduce photographs:
pp. 4, 8, 20 Library of Congress; pp. 6, 14, 22, 24, 30, 33, 35, 38, 41, 42, 44, 46 Bettmann/Corbis; p. 12 The Brett Weston Archive/Corbis; pp. 16, 28, 36, 49, 50, 52, 54, 57 Associated Press, AP; p. 26 Hulton/Archive by Getty Images; p. 58 AFP/Corbis.

Cover photograph: Bettmann/Corbis

Some words are shown in bold, **like this.** You can find out what they mean by looking in the glossary.

# Contents

*Bill Russell was a professional basketball player and coach for almost twenty years. He played for the Boston Celtics from 1956–1969.*

# Introduction

Many great players have done amazing things in basketball. Michael Jordan may have been the best player ever to step onto a court. Magic Johnson, Larry Bird, and Wilt Chamberlain also were great stars. But none of them did what Bill Russell did. They did not even come close.

Bill led his team to the National Basketball Association (NBA) championship eleven times in thirteen years. He was a star for the Boston Celtics from 1956 to 1969. He was not an excellent shooter or flashy player. He did not always score a lot of points. Winning was what mattered to him.

He did everything possible to help his team. He was a skilled passer. His **defense** kept other teams from scoring any easy baskets. And Bill's greatest talent was **rebounding.** When another player missed a shot, Bill wanted to be in the right place to grab the rebound. He did that better than just about anyone. Once he had the **rebound,** Bill could make a basket or pass the ball to a teammate.

*Bill's awesome rebounding skills helped his teams win games and often go all the way to the top.*

The Boston Celtics had never won a championship before Bill joined the team. However, Bill knew how to win big games. In college he played for the University of San Francisco. Bill led the team to 55 wins in a row. The team also won back-to-back national championships. After college, Bill was a star for the 1956 U.S. Olympic basketball team. The team won a gold medal in Melbourne, Australia.

Bill won many honors for his play with the Celtics. He was voted most valuable player five times. He played in the All-Star Game in twelve straight seasons.

It was not always easy for Bill. As a child, he was tall, thin, and clumsy. His older brother was a great athlete, but Bill could not make the team. He was cut from the basketball team every year in junior high school. His luck was no better when he tried out for the football and baseball teams.

He also faced other challenges. He grew up during a time when **discrimination** kept African Americans from having the same freedoms as whites. When he played, he wasn't always welcome in the same places as his white teammates. Sometimes he didn't even feel welcome in Boston.

Bill did things that might have seemed impossible at the time. He led his teams to championship after championship. He became the first African American ever to coach in the NBA. He was the first African American ever elected to the Basketball Hall of Fame. Nobody can match all that.

*Many African Americans fought against segregation in the 1950s and 1960s. These two men carry signs that called for an end to segregation.*

# Chapter 1:
# Family and Youth

Bill Russell's life began far away from the fame and fortune of professional basketball. He grew up poor and survived hard times with his family. Still, he often said his childhood was a happy one. He had his parents to thank for that.

## Early years in the South

Bill was born February 12, 1934, in Monroe, Louisiana. His full name was William Felton Russell. He was the second child of Charles and Katie Russell. Charles worked in a factory that made paper bags. He worked hard but earned little pay.

Back then African Americans rarely got the same chances in life as whites. That was especially true in Louisiana and other states in the South. In those places **segregation** ruled. Segregation was a set of laws that forced people of different races to live separately.

Segregation limited the schools and jobs available to African Americans. In Louisiana, Bill and his older brother, Charlie Jr., went to a school that was only for African-American children. Classes were held in an old barn.

Charles wanted more for his children. He did not believe that he could get ahead in Louisiana. He left his family in search of a better job. Charles made his way to Oakland, California. He got a job in the shipyards there. A shipyard is a place where ships are built and repaired.

Charles worked and saved his money. He needed to save enough to pay for his wife and children to join him in Oakland. When the money came, Katie packed up their things and took her two boys to the train station.

## Life in California

Bill was nine years old when his family moved to California. Things were not easy for the family in Oakland. Their first home was in a house shared by eight families. The house had eight rooms. Each family got one room.

Soon, they moved to an apartment in a new housing project. A project is a group of apartments where the rent is low. Projects are built with money from the government. The project where the Russells lived was integrated. That meant people of all races lived there and were treated the same.

## Leaving segregation behind

Bill Russell's family moved from Louisiana to California in 1943. Bill was nine years old at the time. The long train trip he took with his mother and brother was a hint of what was ahead for them.

In Louisiana, segregation forced all the African-American passengers to stay in certain cars on the train. Segregation was a set of laws that made people of different races live apart. African Americans were not allowed in the dining car, where white passengers could buy snacks and full meals. Bill's mother had to pack enough food for her and the two boys. They rode a train from Louisiana to Little Rock, Arkansas, and then took another train to Saint Louis, Missouri.

Bill got his first taste of life away from segregation when they left Saint Louis. They were no longer in the South. There was no segregation on the trip from Saint Louis to California, where Bill's father awaited. The Russells could move about freely on the train. They could go to any car, including the dining car. They could have their meals along with the white passengers. The freedom helped them to feel good about their move to the West.

Both Charles and Katie worked in the shipyards. One of them worked the day shift. The other worked the night shift. The boys always had at least one of their parents at home to care for them. Bill first learned to play basketball in the project yard.

*The Russells moved to Oakland, California, in 1943. Bill found life in the west coast city to be much different from life in Louisiana.*

Tragedy struck the family in 1946, when Bill was 12 years old. His mother became ill one day and had to be rushed to the hospital. Katie never got over her illness. She died two weeks later from kidney failure. She was only 32.

## Junior high years

Nobody at Hoover Junior High School expected Bill to become a star athlete. If anyone was going to be a star, it was Bill's older brother. Charlie was two years ahead of Bill in school, and Charlie was the best athlete at Hoover. He was the star of the football, basketball, and track teams.

Bill wanted to follow in his brother's footsteps. It wasn't easy. He tried out for the basketball team but was **cut.** That means the coach did not keep him on the team. The same thing happened when he tried out for other teams.

Bill was also doing poorly in his classes. In fact, he almost flunked the eighth grade. That scared him. He started taking his schoolwork more seriously. He began to study hard and improved his grades.

## High school

Bill picked a different high school from his brother's. Charlie went to Oakland Technical High School and was the school's best athlete. Oakland Technical had mostly white students. Bill chose McClymonds High School, which was in his neighborhood. The students were mostly African American.

In 1949 sports were still a challenge for the fifteen-year-old Bill. He tried out for the varsity football team in tenth grade but was cut. He tried out for the varsity basketball team but was cut. He even tried out for the cheerleading squad. No luck.

*Bill was offered a scholarship to play college ball at the University of San Francisco. Scholarships like this were, and still are, very difficult to get.*

Bill thought about giving up on sports, but a teacher helped change his mind. This teacher coached the junior varsity basketball team. He liked Bill and made room for him on the team. The junior varsity team had sixteen players but only fifteen uniforms. Bill had to share a uniform with another boy.

During high school, Bill practiced hard and grew taller each year. He was 6 feet, 1 inch tall in tenth grade. Two years later he was 6 feet, 5 inches. He was skinny, but he worked hard to add muscle to his thin body. Bill finally became a starter for the McClymonds team when he was in twelfth grade. He was a good player but not a star. Few people outside his school had ever heard of him.

His last high school game changed everything. His team was taking on Oakland High, which had a great player named Truman Bruce. Hal DeJulio, a talent scout from the University of San Francisco, went to the game to see Bruce play. However, it was Bill Russell's outstanding performance that impressed DeJulio the most.

Bill scored fourteen points and led his team to a win. After that game, Hal DeJulio decided to offer Bill an athletic scholarship. That meant Bill could go to college for free and play on the basketball team. Bill was surprised and thrilled.

*Bill joined the University of San Francisco Dons in 1952. He helped the team defensively and sometimes scored baskets like this one.*

# Chapter 2: College Years

Star players can often choose among many colleges when they graduate high school. It is common for stars to have their pick of 25 or more colleges. These rare individuals get to decide where to play basketball while they get a free education. Bill was not a star. He had one offer. He took it.

The University of San Francisco was a very small school. It did not even have its own gym. The basketball team practiced at a nearby high school. The school's sports teams were known as the Dons.

The campus was located just a few miles from Bill's home. He knew it was somewhere on the other side of the long bridge that crosses the bay between Oakland and San Francisco. After graduating from high school, Bill crossed the bridge to get a look at the campus. He could not find it. He stopped people on the street to ask for directions. They could not help him. Nobody seemed to know where the tiny campus was.

Of course, Bill finally found the university. In a few years, he put the University of San Francisco on the map. The basketball team made the school famous around the country. Bill was the leader of the team.

## Learning the game

Bill had a lot to learn during his first two years in college. He started school in the fall of 1952, when he was eighteen. He spent his first year practicing with the other **freshmen,** or first-year students. He worked hard to keep on top of his studies. His scholarship gave him a free education, but it did not give him any spending money. Bill worked in the school cafeteria to put a few dollars in his pocket.

He shared a room with a young man named K. C. Jones. Jones was one year ahead of Bill and also played basketball. Jones was very shy. He did not even speak to Bill during the first month they lived together. However, the two became close friends. They wound up playing together for many years to come.

Bill spent long hours on the court. He worked hard to become a better player. He was still growing. He had been 6 feet, 5 inches tall as a high school senior. Two years later, he was 6 feet, 10 inches. He worked hard on his **defense.** He learned how to keep his opponent away from the basket. He showed a talent for rebounding and for leaping high to block shots.

# K. C. Jones

K. C. Jones was more than just a teammate to Bill Russell. He was a friend who was at his side for many great victories. Jones also found success on his own. He was a great player and a winning coach.

Jones and Bill Russell met at the University of San Francisco. They became roommates and teammates in 1952. Jones was a shy and quiet young man. Bill Russell was the opposite. Still, they began a friendship that would last for many years.

Jones played **guard** for the 1955 team that won the national championship. He also played for the 1956 team. But he was not on the court when that team won the championship again. His four years of college playing time ran out before the end of the 1956 season. Both Jones and Bill Russell also played for the 1956 Olympic team. They helped win a gold medal for the United States.

The Boston Celtics picked Bill Russell in the first round of the 1956 **draft**. They chose Jones in the second round. But Jones did not join the Celtics that year. He joined the U.S. Army instead. He spent the next two years in the Army.

When he got out of the Army, Jones went to play for the Celtics. The team won championships in eight of the next nine seasons. Jones played guard for the team. He was not known as a great shooter or scorer. Like his friend Bill Russell, Jones was great on defense. He was an excellent passer. He hustled and worked hard all the time.

After his playing days, Jones became a coach. He worked for several NBA teams in the 1970s and early 1980s. One of those teams was the Boston Celtics. In 1983, the team moved Jones from assistant coach to head coach.

The Celtics won the 1984 NBA championship. That came in Jones's first season as head coach. The team won another championship in 1986. Jones coached the team for five winning seasons. He later coached the Seattle Supersonics. He had a winning record in Seattle from 1990 to 1992. But his team won no championships.

For his achievements as a player, Jones was elected to the Basketball Hall of Fame in 1989.

*Although he was known for his rebounding and defensive skills, Bill also made baskets. He made this one in the 1955 NCAA semifinals.*

In his second year, Bill became the starting **center** for the Dons. The center is usually the tallest player on the team. Each team has five players on the court at a time. The center plays nearest the basket. The center also jumps for the ball that starts the game.

The Dons' season started with a great win, but it went downhill from there. After the first game, Jones became ill.

He had to have an operation and missed the rest of the season. Jones was one of the best players on the team. Without him, the Dons were just a so-so team.

## National champions

Something magical began to happen during Bill's third season with the Dons. Jones was back on the playing court. The team won its first two games. The third game was against the University of California-Los Angeles (UCLA). Bill's team lost to UCLA. The Dons did not lose again for a very long time.

The Dons won every game for the rest of that season. The Final Four was held in Kansas City, Missouri, that year. In the Final Four, the best teams in college basketball play to see who the national champion will be. The Dons beat La Salle in the 1955 championship game.

The winning streak kept going the next season. Bill's team won every game in his final year in college. The Dons went to the Final Four again. They defeated Iowa to win the 1956 national championship.

In the end, the Dons won 55 games in a row. No team had ever done that before. That record was not broken for nearly twenty years.

*Bill was surrounded by fans after he received the MVP Award in the 1956 East-West All-American game.*

Bill made a name for himself as the leader of his team. In 1955 he set the record for the most points scored in the championship tournament. He also was named an **All-American** in 1955 and 1956. That meant he was one of the very top college players in the country. He averaged more than twenty points and twenty **rebounds** per game during college.

## Olympic Gold

In 1956 Bill got a gold medal and a gold ring. The medal was for his play on the U.S. Olympic basketball team. The ring came when he married Rose Swisher, whom he had met at a dance two years earlier.

Bill and his friend K. C. Jones decided to try out for the Olympic team after college. Both of them made the squad. The team practiced during the summer of 1956 and went to the Olympic Games that fall. The games were held in Melbourne, Australia.

The U.S. team was easily the best in the world. It won all eight games it played in the Olympics and claimed the gold medal. Bill had to rush back home after the Olympics. He was due to be married in a few days.

Bill and Rose were married December 10, 1956, in Oakland. The couple had one week for a honeymoon. Then they flew across the country to Boston. Bill joined the Boston Celtics and started his career in professional basketball.

*During a game in 1946, two Celtics players attempt to stop Bob Cluggish of the New York Knickerbockers. In 1946 the Celtics joined the NBA, a newly formed professional basketball league.*

# Chapter 3: Becoming a Pro

The Boston Celtics basketball team began play in 1946. It was part of a brand-new professional basketball league, the NBA. The Celtics had a rough time in the early years. The team was losing on the court and running out of money. In fact, the Celtics came very close to going out of business.

Things were looking up by 1956. The team had a great coach named Red Auerbach. The Celtics were a winning team, but not a great team. Something was missing. Auerbach figured his team needed a big, strong center.

The Celtics traded two players to the Saint Louis Hawks for the chance to **draft** Bill Russell. The draft is a process in which professional teams get to pick from the players coming out of college. Auerbach disagreed with critics who thought Bill would not be a great NBA player. He knew Bill was something special.

*In 1956 Bill signed a contract to become the NBA's highest-paid rookie. Celtics co-owners, Walter Brown and Lou Pieri, look on.*

## A rookie joins the team

Bill had to learn how to play with the pros in a hurry. The Olympics had caused him to miss the first two months of the NBA schedule for 1956–1957. After the Olympics, Bill signed a contract to play for the Celtics. He was paid $19,500 for the year. Bill also asked for a $25,000 bonus to sign a contract. That was a lot of money for a **rookie** player in those days. A rookie is a player in his or her first year.

The Celtics were already a good team. They had many talented players, including a **guard** named Bob Cousy. Guards are usually the smaller, faster players. They dribble the ball up the court and lead their teammates on **offense.** Cousy was one of the best guards in all of basketball. He was lightning quick and dribbled the ball with amazing control. The coach was anxious to add Bill to the mix.

That year, Bill was the only African American on the team. The NBA had several black players, but most of the players in those days were white. The Celtics had one other African-American player before Bill. His name was Chuck Cooper, and he was the first African American ever to play in the league. Cooper played for the Celtics until 1954.

Bill was quiet and careful around his new teammates. He was not sure whether they would accept him. He decided he would not say or do anything to get attention. He wanted to be admired for how he played and who he was. He gained the respect of his teammates quickly. Bill later said that his teammates were more concerned about his basketball skills than the color of his skin.

Bill's life off of the court was not always easy. Some **racist** people from Boston treated Bill and other African Americans poorly. To be racist means to believe one race is better than another. Bill often encountered racism in Boston. Some white people tried to prevent Bill from moving into their neighborhood.

*Bill was one of the only African-American players in the NBA when he joined the Celtics in 1956.*

When they were not successful, they had a friend purchase the house in their Boston neighborhood so that Bill could not. This made Bill angry. He knew it was not right that he was being judged by the color of his skin. Unfortunately, it would be many years before people's racist attitudes changed for the better.

## The first championship

Coach Auerbach had some advice for his newest player. He told Bill not to worry about scoring a lot of points. Auerbach said he would count **rebounds** for Bill the way he would count baskets for another player. He wanted the rookie to focus on **defense** and rebounding. Bill did just that. When another player missed a shot, chances were good that Bill would grab the rebound. He took in more than nineteen rebounds a game that year.

Bill also played defense like nobody before him. When players are on defense, they each defend against one player on the other team. They try to stop that person from scoring a basket. They want to keep the ball away from the players on the other team. Most coaches back then told their players to keep their feet on the ground when they were on defense. Bill did not work that way. He buzzed around the court. He leapt high to block shots. Often, he batted the ball to a waiting teammate, and the Celtics were off and running in the other direction.

The Celtics made it to the NBA finals that year with Bill leading the way. The team took on the Saint Louis Hawks in a seven-game series. The teams split the first six games. Everything was riding on the seventh game. The Celtics fought through two overtime periods and won the game. The Celtics were the 1956–1957 NBA champions.

*Bill, furthest on the left in the back row, was an important player in the Celtics'*
*victories over the Lakers for the 1959 NBA championship.*

# Chapter 4:
# The Great Defender

Bill's second season with the Celtics seemed as though it would end like the first. The team was playing wonderfully and steamed its way back to the NBA finals. Again, the Celtics had to take on the Saint Louis Hawks, who had put up a tough fight the year before.

It had been a great year for Bill. He became one of the league's top players. His defense put fear into opposing teams. He also showed himself to be a talented player on offense. A team is on offense when it has the ball and is trying to score a basket. After his second season, Bill was voted the **Most Valuable Player (MVP)** of the NBA.

Still, the season ended unhappily. Bill twisted his ankle in the third game of the championship series. With him injured, the Celtics lost the 1957–1958 championship to the Hawks in six games.

## Beginning of an era

The loss in the 1958 finals was a disappointing end to a great season. Bill and his teammates wanted to get the champion title back the next year. The Celtics did that, but it was only the beginning.

For the next eight seasons, the Celtics ruled the NBA. Bill was in the middle of it all. He was the team's leader. He was the first African-American superstar in the NBA. And he was a whole new kind of player. He did not play for himself. Bill played selflessly and focused on making the team play well together.

The Celtics made it to the NBA finals after the 1958–1959 season. They took on the Minneapolis Lakers, but it was no contest. Bill's team won the series by four games to zero. Bill set a record for **rebounds** in the finals. He grabbed 29 rebounds per game.

When the Celtics won in 1959, the team started the longest championship streak ever in the NBA. In fact, it was the longest streak in any professional sport. The Celtics won eight championships in a row. No team had done that before. No team has even come close to doing it since.

## Wilt Chamberlain (1936–1999)

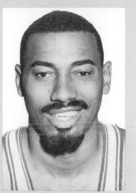

Wilt Chamberlain was another one of the brightest stars of his time. He played against Bill many times during their careers. Bill's teams won many more championships, but that cannot take away from Chamberlain's amazing achievements.

Chamberlain was a huge man. He stood 7 feet, 1 inch and weighed 275 pounds. But he was still smooth and graceful. He was known for his jump shot and his finger-roll **lay-ins.** For a finger roll, the player leaps up like he's going to dunk the ball. Instead of dunking, though, he lets the ball roll gently off his fingers and into the hoop. He also blocked shots and grabbed even more rebounds than Bill Russell. In fact, Chamberlain had more **rebounds** than anyone in NBA history.

Chamberlain was the **Rookie** of the Year in 1960. He played for three different teams during his fourteen years in the NBA. He was named the **Most Valuable Player (MVP)** four times. He led the league in scoring in seven seasons. He was the only player to score 100 points in a single game.

Sadly, Wilt Chamberlain died from a heart attack in 1999 at the age of 63.

## A new kind of star

Bill was not the kind of player most people think of as a superstar. He was not a great shooter. He did not score a lot of points. He was better at stopping the other team from scoring. He did that better than anyone.

Bill could shut down the other team's **center,** but his **defense** did not stop at that. He had control of the **lane.** A lane is a rectangular area from the basket to the free-throw line. Opposing players were taking a chance if they tried to dribble in close to the basket to shoot a **lay-up.** Bill was often there to block the shot.

He moved with amazing speed for a man his size. Sportswriters often said Bill was as quick and smooth as a cat. If another player dribbled to the basket, Bill would leave his man. He would slide across the lane and leap high for the block. If the player somehow got the shot over him, Bill was ready to snatch the **rebound.**

During the 1958–1959 season, Bill led the NBA in rebounds. He grabbed 23 rebounds per game. The NBA did not keep track of blocked shots back then. If it had, Bill surely would have had the most.

A former Celtics player named Don Nelson explained Bill's skills. Nelson said there are two kinds of superstars. The first makes himself look great. The second makes his team look great. Bill was the best of the second kind, Nelson said.

## The streak goes on

After winning in 1959, the Celtics were after the championship again in the 1959–1960 season. But it wasn't going to be easy. The NBA was full of talented teams, and a **rookie** star was rising.

*Bill Russell was not as big as Wilt Chamberlain. But Bill's defense was tough enough to make the NBA star miss this shot in a 1960 game.*

Wilt Chamberlain had started playing for the Philadelphia Warriors. Chamberlain was a giant of a man. Yet he moved with speed and shot the ball well. In his first year, Chamberlain won both Rookie of the Year and **Most Valuable Player (MVP)** in the NBA.

*Bill received the Player of the Year award from NBA commissioner Walter Kennedy during halftime of the 1964 All-Star Game.*

However, Bill was the one with the championship trophy. The Celtics beat the Warriors in the playoffs. Then the Celtics went to the finals against the Hawks. Bill took control in the seventh game of the championship series. He had 22 points and 35 **rebounds.** The Celtics won 122 to 103.

Behind Bill, the Celtics piled up the championships. Bill was voted **MVP** for the 1960–1961 season, and the Celtics won the championship. Bill's best season for scoring came in 1961–1962. He scored about 19 points a game that year. Chamberlain was the NBA's top scorer. He amazed fans by scoring more than 50 points |a game. However, the Celtics won the championship, and Bill was voted MVP.

Bill took the MVP again in 1962–1963, and the Celtics won again. The Celtics' talented **guard** Bob Cousy retired after the 1962–1963 season. A new player named John Havlicek joined the team, and he became another Celtics star.

Bill said the Celtics' best team played in the 1963–1964 season. Along with Havlicek and Bill, the Celtics also had great players such as Sam Jones and K. C. Jones. Jones, Bill's old friend from college, had joined the Celtics in 1958. The Celtics easily won the championship in 1964. They were the first team in any professional sport to win six titles in a row.

Bill did not let people's racism prevent him from being a fantastic basketball player. The Celtics won two more championships. Things changed for Bill after the eighth straight win, though. He and his teammates had made history with their great performance on the court. It was time for Bill to make history in another way.

*Coach Auerbach had no question who should replace him as coach of the Celtics in 1966. Here, he gave Bill a hug at a press conference.*

# Chapter 5:
# The Player-Coach

Coach Red Auerbach was already a legend by 1966. His team had won eight straight championships. He was ready to retire and to pick somebody else to lead the Celtics. Auerbach knew exactly who should replace him.

The old coach asked his star player, Bill Russell, to take the job. Bill gladly accepted. He became the first African American ever to coach a team in the NBA. He also continued to play for the team. That made him a player-coach. It was unusual for a player to be made the coach of a team. It is still unusual, but it happens from time to time in professional sports.

Bill held the job for three years. His team went through highs and lows during that time. His first season as coach ended badly, but the Celtics bounced back next season under their new coach.

## The streak ends

Bill was under a lot of pressure when the 1966–1967 season began. He had big shoes to fill. After all, he was taking charge of the most successful team ever in pro sports. He also was the first African American to coach in the league. Many **racist** white people believed that black people could not be good leaders. Bill wanted to prove them wrong and open the door for other African Americans.

The Celtics won 60 games and lost only 21 that year. Bill was an excellent coach. He emphasized selflessness and teamwork on the court. However, the Philadelphia 76ers had a better year. Their record was 68 and 13. The 76ers had Wilt Chamberlain to lead the way. Chamberlain had left the Warriors after more than five years in the NBA. He became the 76ers' star.

The teams met in the playoffs for the chance to play in the championship series. Chamberlain and the 76ers were too much for the Celtics that year. The 76ers won the playoff series in five games. Philadelphia won the championship that year, and Chamberlain was voted the league **MVP.**

The streak was over for the Celtics. However, good times were still ahead for Bill and his teammates.

## Making a comeback

Bill's body was showing wear and tear at the start of the 1967–1968 season. He was 33 years old. It was only his second

*Bill battles Wilt Chamberlain for the rebound in game four of the 1967 NBA Championships. The Celtics won 121-117.*

*Bill felt the pain when Chamberlain came down on his back in game five of the 1967 NBA Championships. The Philadelphia 76ers won.*

year as coach, but it was his twelfth as a player. He had worked hard during each of those seasons, and his knees had taken a beating. Often he could not play during practice. He could only rest his body and coach the other players. However, he was always ready for the games.

The Celtics were after another championship. Bill knew they would have to get past the 76ers first. The two teams again met in the playoffs. The winner would move ahead to play the Los Angeles

Lakers in the NBA finals. (The Lakers had moved from Minneapolis to Los Angeles in 1960.) The playoff battle between the Celtics and the 76ers turned out to be a great one.

Against the 76ers, Bill showed he could still do things that seemed impossible. The teams split the first six games. Everything was riding on the seventh game. With 34 seconds left in the game, the Celtics were leading 97 to 95, but the 76ers were making a charge. Then Bill did his thing. He made a free throw to give his team a bigger lead. Then he blocked a shot by a 76ers player and

## No autographs, please

As a player, Bill Russell did not give autographs. He made no exceptions, even for teammates. Some fans were angry when Bill turned down their requests for an autograph, but the Celtics' star had a good reason.

Bill thought he could be closer to fans by not signing autographs. If someone asked for an autograph, Bill would politely say no. But he was happy to shake hands, and he would gladly chat for a moment or two. He liked to have real interactions with his fans, rather than just signing a piece of paper and moving on.

In recent years, Bill has surprised fans by giving a small number of autographs. He signs some each year, and many are sold in sports memorabilia stores.

*Bill and player Emmette Bryant headed to the showers after the Celtics defeated the Los Angeles Lakers for their 11th NBA Championship.*

grabbed a **rebound** after a missed shot. He passed the ball to Sam Jones, who made a basket to put the game away. Bill did all that in 34 seconds. The Celtics won 100 to 96.

In the finals, the Celtics beat the Lakers easily. It was the tenth NBA title for the Celtics since Bill had joined the team. And he had one more to go.

# Going out on top

During the 1968–1969 season, Bill was 35 years old. His playing days were nearly over, and his team was far from great. The Celtics won only 48 games that year and lost 34. They barely qualified for the playoffs. However, the Celtics knew what to do once they got there.

Boston surprised fans by making it back to the championship series. Most people expected them to lose early in the playoffs. In the finals, the Celtics again played the Lakers, but it was not the same team they had beaten the year before. Wilt Chamberlain had joined the Lakers that year, and he was still the NBA's greatest scorer. The series went to the seventh game. Bill and the Celtics pulled off an **upset.** They were champions again. The series showed the difference between Chamberlain and Bill. Chamberlain scored a lot of points, but Bill won a lot of championships.

Bill retired shortly after the 1968–1969 season. He gave up his duties as both a player and a coach. Bill had been the star of the Celtics for thirteen seasons. He had helped the team win eleven championships during that time. Chamberlain played for fourteen seasons and won only two championships.

When a team wins the championship, each player is given a ring as an award. Bill had more rings than he had fingers. No player in the history of basketball has come close to matching that. Even the great Michael Jordan won only six rings.

*Bill had reason to laugh after he coached the Seattle Supersonics to their first NBA playoff game in 1975.*

# Chapter 6:
# Later Life

Bill Russell's time with the Celtics came to an end in 1969. He was 35 years old when he left basketball. Without him, the Celtics struggled. They failed to make the playoffs the next season. The Celtics would be a great team again someday, but Bill could not be replaced easily.

At home, he had a young daughter to keep him busy. Karen Russell was in elementary school in 1969. She was the only child of Bill and his wife Rose. For many years, basketball had kept Bill apart from his daughter. The Celtics had to travel all around the country during the season. However, the family had plenty of time together now that Bill's playing days were over.

Bill was no longer a Celtic, but he did not leave basketball behind for good. Within a few years, he was back at work as a coach. He also spent many years as a television commentator. A commentator describes the action when a game is on TV.

## Return to coaching

Bill coached for two teams after retiring from the Celtics. He worked first for the Seattle Supersonics and later for the Sacramento Kings. He had some success in Seattle but very littlein Sacramento.

The Sonics had never made the playoffs before they hired Bill. He was given two jobs. He coached the team, and he was the general manager. The general manager decides which players will be on the team and gets them to sign contracts. Bill's job was to build a winner.

Bill was hired by the Sonics in 1973 and stayed with the team until 1977. The team's record during his four seasons was 162 wins and 166 losses. However, he led the Sonics to the playoffs for the first time. He tried to show the players how to work together and play as a team. Two years after he left, the Sonics won the NBA championship. Many people gave Bill credit for putting together that championship team.

In 1987 he returned to the sidelines. He coached the Kings during the 1987–1988 season, but it was an unhappy time. His team struggled. They won 17 games and lost 41 under Bill. He was fired. It was disappointing for Bill, but it could not sour his great career.

*Bill and K. C. Jones, former Celtics teammates, share a laugh before the start of a Celtics-Kings basketball game in 1988. Bill coaches the Sacramento Kings and K. C. coaches the Boston Celtics.*

*The jerseys of Wilt Chamberlain and Bill Russell hang side-by-side in the Basketball Hall of Fame in Springfield, Massachusetts.*

## Honors for a star

Two major honors came to Bill soon after he retired as a player. First, the Celtics retired his number. In 1975 he was **inducted** to the Basketball Hall of Fame. To be inducted means to formally be made part of a group. He became the first African American to make it into the Hall of Fame.

Bill wore number six for the Celtics. In 1972 the team hung his number from the rafters of Boston Garden, the team's famous old arena. No Celtics player will ever again wear that number. Retiring a number is a way of honoring a player. It is like saying no player could ever match what that person did for the team.

Being the first African American elected to the Hall of Fame was also an honor. However, Bill thought it was wrong that no other African Americans had been in the Hall before him. He believed it was a sign that black people were still not being treated fairly, both inside and outside of the world of sports. Bill decided to protest that unfairness. He did not attend the 1975 ceremony where he was inducted into the Hall of Fame.

## Family life

During his retirement, Bill made family a major part of his life. He wanted his daughter to have a happy childhood and go off to college. When he was a child, Bill's mother wanted her two sons to go to college more than anything else.

Before she died, his mother, Katie Russell, asked his father to promise that the boys would go to college. It wasn't easy for Charles Russell to keep that promise. He was raising his children alone, and the family did not have a lot of money. In the end, both boys did graduate from college. Charlie Jr. became a social worker and playwright, a person who writes plays.

*Bill's former coach, Red Auerbach, gives him a hug during a tribute to the Celtics legend at Boston's Fleet Center in May of 1999.*

Bill carried the college dream for his own daughter. Karen left home in 1980 and began college at Georgetown University, in Washington, D.C. Later, she graduated from law school at Harvard University, which is one of the best and toughest law schools in the United States.

## Lasting fame

Today, Bill remains a popular but private person. Today, he is beloved in Boston, where he led the Celtics to eleven championships. Banners for each of those championships hang in the rafters of a new arena. The Celtics left the Boston Garden and moved into the new Fleet Center in 1995.

Thirty years after his last game as a player, Bill was honored by the Celtics in a public ceremony. In 1972 there was only a small, private ceremony when Bill's number was retired. Because of his experiences in Boston, Bill had not wanted a public event. He had never felt welcomed or accepted in Boston because he was an African American.

In 1999 the team held a special celebration at its new arena. Thousands of fans cheered when Bill's number was re-retired. Times had finally changed. Basketball fans now recognized Bill's outstanding contributions to basketball instead of the color of his skin.

Many of his old teammates and opponents also came to applaud Bill. Even Wilt Chamberlain was there. Red Auerbach, who had coached Bill for many years, spoke to the crowd in Boston. "Bill Russell is the greatest winner ever to play the game," Auerbach said.

*Bill answers questions after working out with the Celtics in October of 1999. He occasionally works out and helps with the team.*

# Chapter 7:
# His Place in History

There are many ways to measure a player's greatness. By some standards, Bill Russell does not rank even close to the top. In other ways, nobody can match Bill's achievements.

Often players are judged by the number of points they score. Bill scored a lot of baskets for the Celtics, but he was never a leader in the league. He scored 15 points per game during his career. Wilt Chamberlain scored more than 30 points per game, and he held the record for a long time. Michael Jordan scored more than 31 points per game.

In **rebounding,** Bill was among the best of all time. He grabbed a total of 21,620 rebounds in his career. Only Wilt Chamberlain had more. Bill holds several rebounding records. For example, he ranks first in rebounds during the playoffs. He also was the first player to get 50 rebounds in one game. He led the NBA in rebounding four times during his thirteen seasons.

Bill liked to measure his success by how his team did. The Celtics, of course, did very well. The team's eight straight championships set a record that will be very hard to break. Bill helped the team make winning seem routine. He led the team for thirteen years, and the Celtics won eleven titles.

Most basketball experts give Bill much of the credit for those championships. In 1980, Bill was voted the greatest player in the history of the NBA by the Professional Basketball Writers Association. He also received a special honor in 1996. The NBA was celebrating its 50th anniversary that year. The league named

a team of the greatest players from those 50 years. Bill was on that all-time greatest team, along with players such as Wilt Chamberlain, Michael Jordan, and Magic Johnson.

## Opening the door

Bill Russell was the first African American to coach a team in the NBA. He was a success in many ways. The Celtics won two championships under his coaching. But he did something more important than winning. He opened the door for other African Americans to coach in the league. It's now fairly common for African Americans to coach in pro basketball. During the 2001–2002 season, thirteen NBA teams had African-American coaches.

*Bill, the only five-time winner of the Most Valuable Player award, presents the MVP trophy to Michael Jordan in 1998. Bill is considered one of the greatest players from the NBA's first 50 years.*

*In May 2000, basketball legend Bill Russell presented Alonzo Mourning of the Miami Heat with the NBA's Defensive Player of the Year Award.*

Maybe the most important thing Bill did was to change the way people thought about basketball. He changed how the position of **center** was played. He was not a tall, clumsy player like many centers before him. He was not a slow-footed giant who bounded around the court. He was large, strong, quick, and graceful. Great centers such as David Robinson and Hakeem Olajuwon followed in his footsteps.

For Bill, the greatest thrill in basketball was getting an entire team working together. "To me, one of the most beautiful things was to see a group of men coordinating their efforts toward a common goal," he once wrote. "I tried to do that; we all tried to do that on the Celtics. I think we succeeded."

# Glossary

**all-American**  basketball players chosen as the best in the United States

**athletic scholarship**  college education given free of charge to student-athletes who play on a college team

**center**  player who jumps for the jump ball at the beginning of the game. The center usually plays nearest the basket during the game.

**cut**  being left off a team after trying out

**draft**  process in which professional teams take turns picking from the players coming out of college

**defense**  what the team that does not have the ball does to prevent the other team from scoring

**discrimination**  treating a person unfairly because the person is different in some way

**freshman**  student in first year of college or high school

**guard**  player who dribbles the ball up the court and leads his or her team when on offense. The guard usually plays farthest from the basket.

**integrated**  open equally to people of all races

**inducted**  to be formally made part of a group or organization

**lane**  area that is 12 feet wide and runs from under the basket to the free-throw line

**lay-up**  shot made from near the basket by playing the ball off the backboard

**most valuable player (MVP)**  an award given to a member of a sports team who has been the greatest help to the team during a certain time period

**offense**  team that has the ball and is trying to score a basket

**projects**  group of apartments with low rent. Projects are built with money from the government.

**racist**  person who thinks that one race is better than another

**rebound**  catch the ball off the backboard or rim after a missed shot

**rookie**  player in his or her first year

**segregation**  forcing people of different races to live apart

**upset**  surprise win from a team that was expected to lose

**shipyard**  place where ships are built or repaired

# Timeline

1934: Bill is born in Monroe, Louisiana.

1952: Bill graduates from high school, begins school at University of San Francisco on an **athletic scholarship.**

1955: University of San Francisco basketball team wins the national championship; team begins a 55-game winning streak.

1956: University of San Francisco wins national championship; Bill is named college player of the year; leads U.S. Olympic team to gold medal; marries Rose Swisher; joins the Boston Celtics.

1957: Celtics win NBA championship.

1958: Bill leads NBA in **rebounds** and is voted league **MVP;** Celtics lose in NBA finals.

1959–1966: Celtics win NBA championship.

1968: Celtics win NBA championship; Bill named Sportsman of the Year.

1969: Celtics win NBA championship; Bill retires after season.

1972: Celtics retire Bill's number (6).

1974: Bill is hired by Seattle Supersonics as coach and general manager.

1975: Bill is **inducted** into the Basketball Hall of Fame.

1977: Bill leaves Supersonics after four seasons.

1980: The Professional Basketball Writers Association names Bill the greatest player in the history of the NBA.

1987: Bill is hired to coach Sacramento Kings.

1988: Bill is fired by the Kings.

1996: Bill is named to NBA 50th Anniversary All-Time Team.

1999: In a public ceremony, Bill's number is re-retired.

# Further Information

## Further reading

Hayhurst, Chris. *Bill Russell.* New York: Rosen Publishing, 2001.

Knapp, Ron. *Top 10 Professional Basketball Coaches.* Berkeley Heights, NJ: Enslow, 1998.

McKissack, Frederick L. *Black Hoops: The History of African Americans in Basketball.* New York: Scholastic, 1999.

## Addresses

Boston Celtics
151 Merrimac Street
Boston, MA 02114
*Write here for more information about current and past Celtic players and coaches.*

Naismith Memorial Basketball Hall of Fame
1000 West Columbus Avenue
Springfield, MA 01105
*Write here to learn more about memorable events in the history of basketball.*

University of San Francisco Athletic Department
2130 Fulton Street
San Francisco, CA 94117
*Write here to learn more about the history of their basketball program, including the years that Bill Russell played for them.*

# Index